J IS FOR
JUNETEENTH

Jamariah Cross, Kimani Prince
and Ariyah Webster

Planting People Growing Justice Press
P.O. Box 131894
Saint Paul, MN 55113
www.ppgjli.org

Printed and bound in China
LCCN: 2023932852
2-9781959223412-01/04/2024

DEDICATIONS

Jamariah Cross:
I want to dedicate this book to everyone. Please learn about my culture and others. They are all different and special.

Kimani Prince:
This is dedicated to kids my age, to learn more about Juneteenth.

Ariyah Webster:
This is dedicated to all people, hoping they will try to understand and appreciate all cultures.

J is for Justice.

Justice for the slaves finally came when the Union Army arrived in Galveston, Texas and shared the news that they were free.

U is for the Union Army.

The Union Army spread the word about independence throughout Texas.

N is for Nineteenth.

Slaves did not find out about their freedom until two years after the Civil War ended on June 19th, 1865.

E is for Equality.

Equality for all means the promise of liberty and freedom.

T is for Tell.

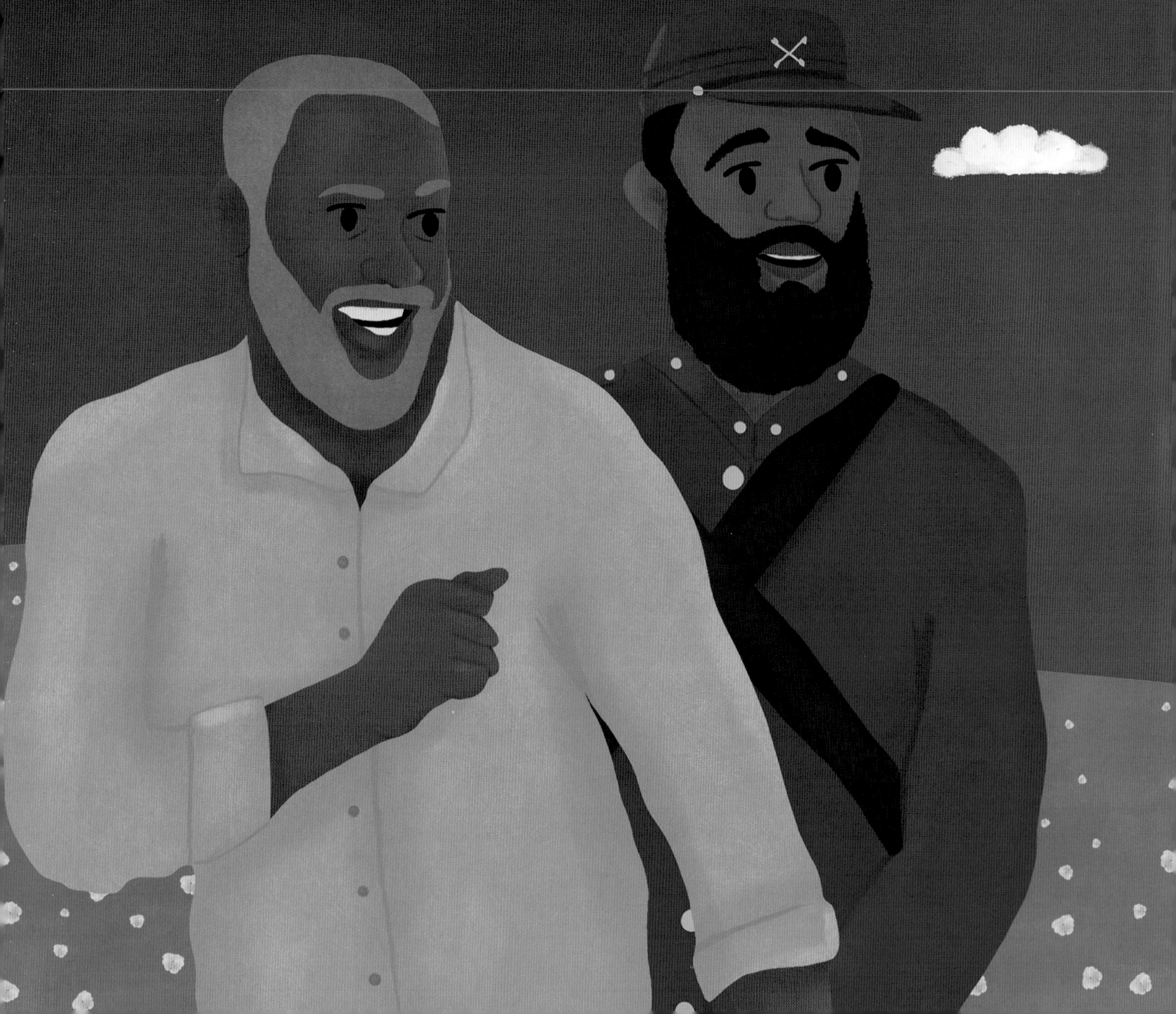

Union soldiers were sent to tell the slaves that the promise of freedom had arrived and they rejoiced.

E is for Emancipation.

Even though they did not know they were free, they had a dream to be emancipated — free one day.

E is for Excitement.

Freed slaves were excited for the future of new generations to come.

N is for Never Gave Up.

Enslaved people were strong and never gave up.

T is for Texas.

Texas was the first state to make Juneteenth a holiday.

H is for Holiday.

Juneteenth is a holiday that is celebrated on June 19th each year across the United States.

J is for Juneteenth.

JUNET